HORRORGAMI

SPOOKY
PAPERFOLDING
JUST FOR FUN

RICHARD SAUNDERS • BRIAN MACKNESS

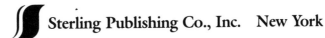
Sterling Publishing Co., Inc.   New York

Library of Congress Cataloging-in-Publication Data

Saunders, Richard, 1965–
    Horrorgami : spooky paperfolding just for fun / Richard Saunders
& Brian Mackness.
       p.   cm.
    Reprint. Originally published: Melbourne : Lothian Pub. Co., 1990.
    Includes index.
    ISBN 0-8069-8480-5
    1. Origami.   I. Mackness, Brian.   II. Title.
TT870.S285   1991
736′.982—dc20
                                        91-20005
                                          CIP

10 9 8 7 6 5 4 3 2 1

Published in 1991 by Sterling Publishing Company, Inc.
387 Park Avenue South, New York, N.Y. 10016
Originally published in Australia by Lothian Publishing
Company Pty. Ltd. Text © 1990 by Brian Mackness.
Models, folding instructions, and original illustrations
© 1990 by Richard Saunders
Distributed in Canada by Sterling Publishing
% Canadian Manda Group, P.O. Box 920, Station U
Toronto, Ontario, Canada M8Z 5P9
Manufactured in the United States of America
All rights reserved

Sterling ISBN 0-8069-8480-5

CONTENTS

Introduction

Beware all who enter the pages of this book. Take heed of the warning that has been scratched into the paper . . . the ghoulish creations may be of paper but they carry a potent spell. Only the very strongest will survive the spell of **Horrorgami**.

Descend into the crypt and gaze into the glassy stare of the **Zombie**. Feel the sticky strands of the **Spider's web** as you push against it on your way into the **Grave**. Be on your guard as you hear the distant howl of the **Werewolf**. Remember not to be late, you have an appointment with **Dracula**.

There are even real animals here that scare people. So if you can stop shaking long enough, pick up your paper and begin folding. But never, whatever you do, never ever fold in the dark. Why??? Because you won't be able to see what you are doing! Bor ha ha ha ha ha ha!

Richard Saunders
Brian Mackness

Reader's Note

For most models very thin, strong paper, like wrapping paper or origami paper, works best. When directions call for a square of paper, begin with a perfect square. Also, make sure your creases are sharp, clean and perfectly even. Use your thumbnail to press in final creases.

Basic Folds and Bases

There are many folds and bases (pre-folded points) used in origami. To cut down on repetitive instructions we have included this guide to some of the more common folds and bases used in this book. Study each one carefully. Some of the folds are marked by symbols. Learn to recognize them because they feature in many of the diagrams.

Folds

1
Valley fold

2
Mountain fold

3
Turn the model over

4
Rabbit's-ear fold

5
Enlarged view

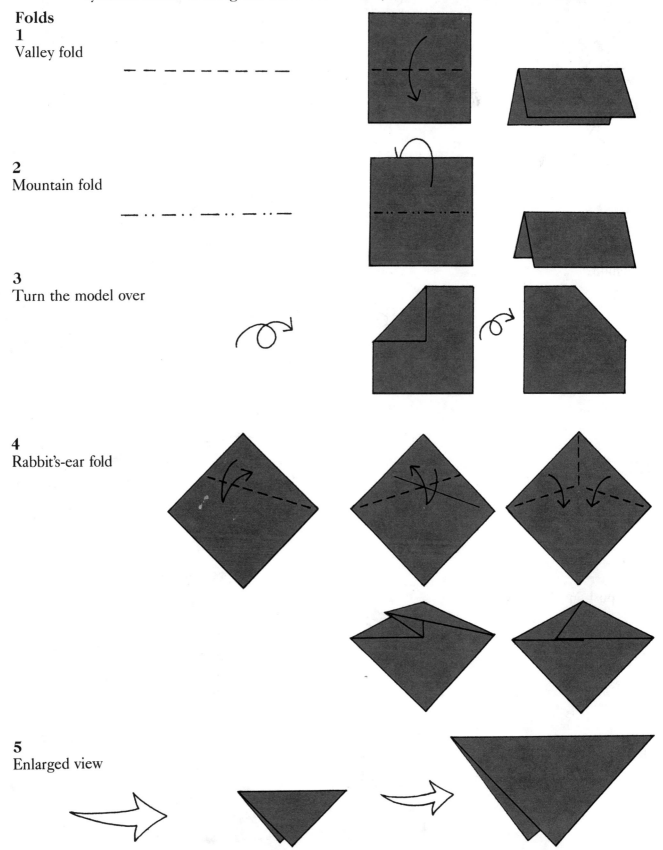

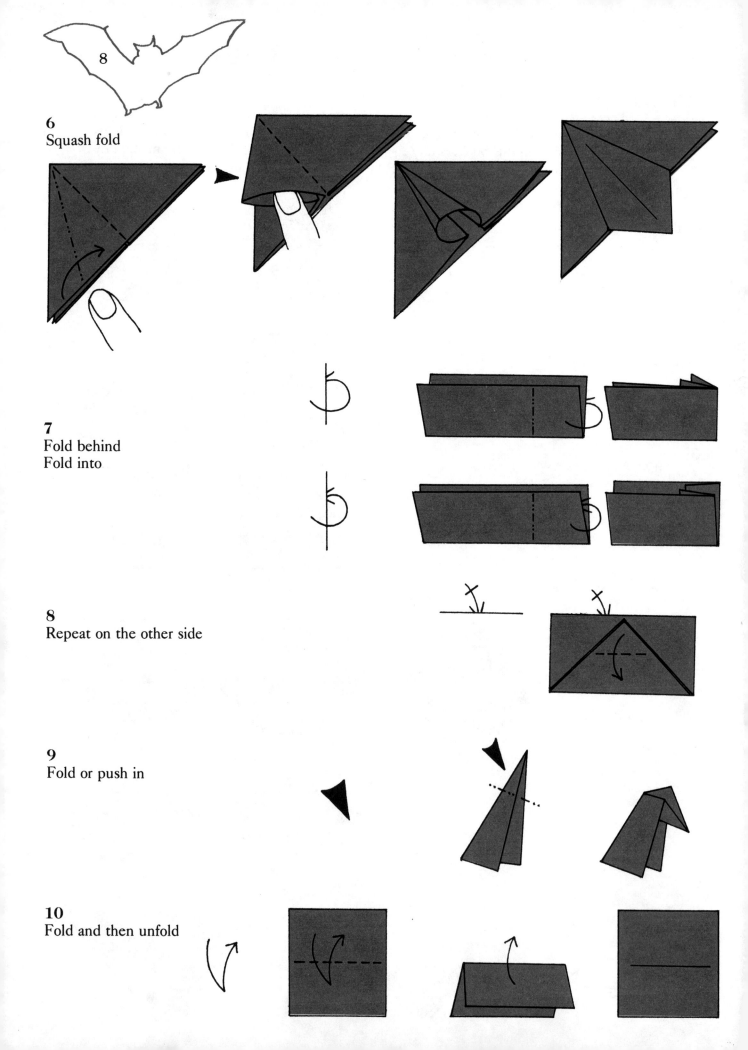

6
Squash fold

7
Fold behind
Fold into

8
Repeat on the other side

9
Fold or push in

10
Fold and then unfold

Flying Ghost

Folding Instructions

Start with the bird base.

1
Reach in and grab the two inner flaps marked.

2
Holding these flaps, pull them apart until your base is stretched out.

3
This is how your model should look. Fold the lower point up to meet the top one. You should be able to squash your model flat.

4
Rabbit's ear fold the front section down to the left. Repeat on the other side: turn your model over, rabbit's ear fold the front section down to the left and turn the model over again.

5
This is how your model should look. Take the front point on the right and squash fold it flat.

6
Fold this new section in half from left to right.

7
Now repeat steps 5 and 6 on the left point.

8
Fold the front right flap over to the left. Turn your model over and repeat on the other side. Turn the model over again.

9
Fold the front flap up.

10
Crimp fold the bottom section and the top as shown.

11
Fold the model in half from left to right.

12
Reverse fold the top point to the left. Crimp the ends of the arms to form hands. Grab the bottom section and pull it to the left. Make a small hole in the back of the model to tie a length of string.

13
Make up more ghosts to create a mobile.

GRAVE

A grave is usually a hole dug in the ground where a dead person is to be buried. It can also be the mound of earth or monument over the top of the body, or even the place where a body is put to rest—for instance, the sea is sometimes called "a watery grave."

Many gruesome stories have been told about graves. A grave is supposed to be where a corpse may rise, breaking through coffin and soil to free itself. Graves and graveyards are also popular meeting places of witches, ghosts and evil spirits.

But not only the dead disturb graves. About 150 years ago, some evil doctors started stealing bodies out of their graves so that they could carry out experiments or dissections. These doctors became known as "grave-robbers." The most famous of these was the legendary Dr. Frankenstein, who robbed graves to create his monster.

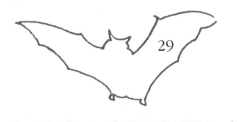

Folding Instructions

1

Start with a piece of paper 8½ × 3½ inches. Fold it in half from top to bottom; then unfold it. Turn the paper over.

2

Fold the top and bottom edges into the middle.

3

Note the corners marked *X*. Fold the right half of the model up at right angles to the left half, opening out the right half as you go.

4

This is how your model should look from the top and the side. Take the left half and fold it under the upright section to the right, as shown.

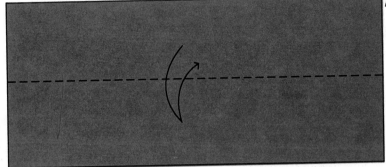

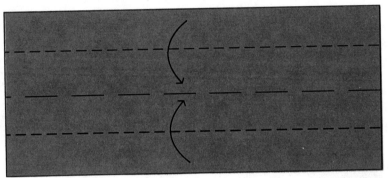

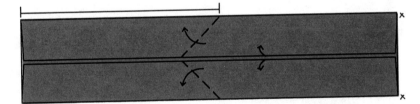

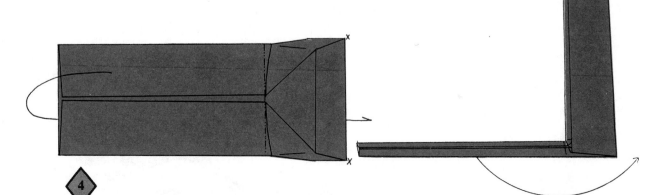

30

5

You will see that the grave is now taking shape. Note the circled area. Turn the model over.

6

This is the circled area. Fold up the end section, at the same time pushing in the corners.

7

This is a close up of one of the corners from the inside. Squash fold it against the sides.

8

Now fold the top of the squashed corner down over the outside. Repeat steps 7 and 8 on the other corner.

9

This is how the under side should look. Turn the model over.

10

Turn the model so that the back of the upright section is facing you. Fold the top and bottom corners of the upright section in as shown.

11

Fold the top edge down a little way.

12

Now fold down the new top corners. Turn the model around.

13

Your grave is now finished. You can add to it by cutting out a small cross or whatever you like and gluing it to the headstone.

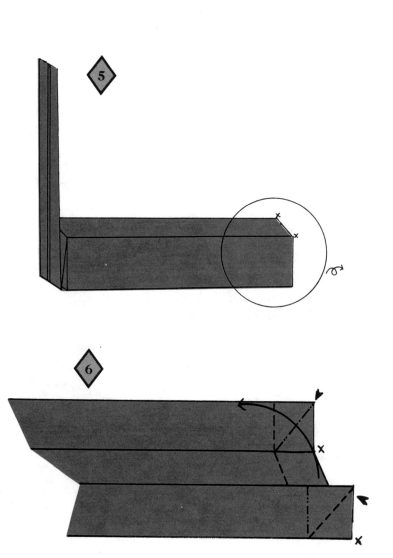

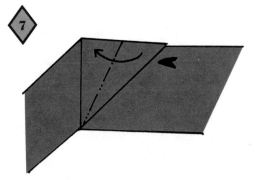

GRIM REAPER

The "Grim Reaper" is a symbol of death. People pictured Death personified as a tall skeleton, gleaming pale against a black robe. It carried a scythe in one bony hand, which it used to "reap" those souls it wanted to take into the world of the dead.

No one could hear the Grim Reaper's ghostly footsteps or predict who would be its next victim. It usually appeared when a lot of people were sick or starving. The dark figure of the Grim Reaper was often seen in paintings, particularly during the Middle Ages, when whole villages died of the plague or "black death."

No pleas or bargains could be made with the Grim Reaper. If those skeletal fingers touched your skin, you were doomed. Many people who were young and healthy refused to believe in its power. But Death always wins in the end.

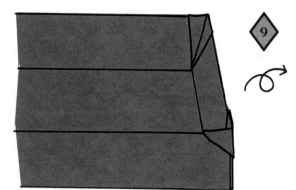

9

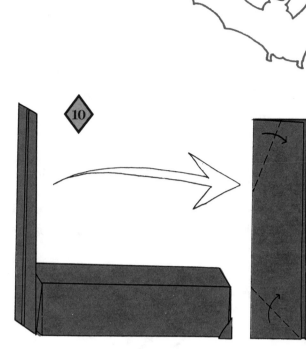

10

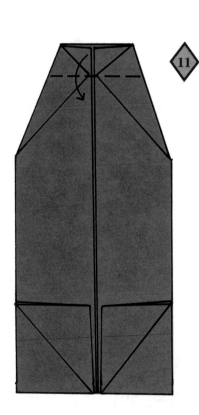

11

31

12

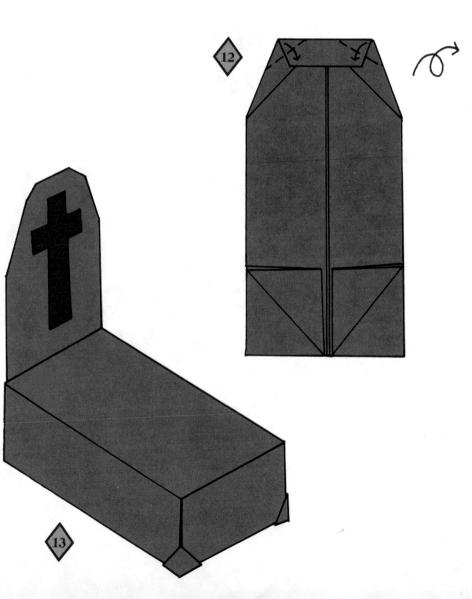

13

11
Inside reverse fold

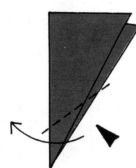

12
Outside reverse fold

13
Hold here

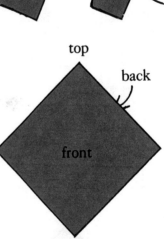

14
Positions on model

top

back

front

bottom

15
X-ray view or guidelines

. . . .

16
Crimp fold

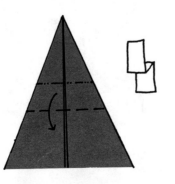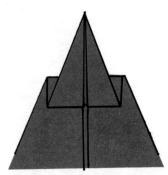

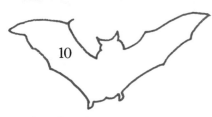

Starter Base

Folding Instructions

1
Fold a piece of paper in half from side to side and then unfold it.

2
Fold it in half from top to bottom and then unfold. Turn over.

3
Repeat steps 1 and 2 but fold on the diagonal.

4
Grab left and right corners and bring together on bottom corner. Then place top corner on them to form the diamond shape base shown. We will call this the starter base.

5
This is how it should look halfway through.

6
This is the finished starter base.

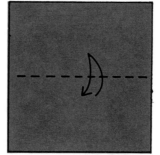

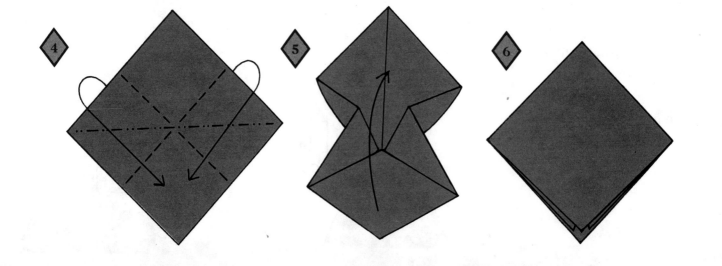

Bird Base

Folding Instructions

The bird base is the foundation of many origami models so you should practice making it until you get it right.

Begin by folding the starter base.

1
Now fold the front two corners into the middle as shown.

2
Fold the top over into the middle as shown.

3
Unfold all the folds you have just made in 1 and 2.

4
Pull up the front flap as shown, folding in the side along the creases, making sure edges meet in the middle.

5
This shows how it should look halfway through.

6
Fold the top of the diamond to the bottom.

7
Turn over and repeat steps 1 to 6 on the other side. Once you have done this you will have a bird base ready for some really exciting creations.

8
This is the finished base.

Frog Base

Folding Instructions

Begin by folding the starter base.

1
Squash fold each of the four sections.

2
Lift the top flap back slightly, at the same time pushing in flap edges to align with the middle. Repeat this for each section.

3
This is your completed frog base.

BATTLE AXE

Battle axes were lethal weapons, as many ancient warriors discovered. A battle axe was one of the best ways to inflict injury upon an enemy. After all, very few people could withstand being smashed by a huge metal and stone axe. Even more terrifying was the "hiss" made by the razor-sharp weapon as it was swung through the air.

The people who really gave the battle axe its feared name were the Vikings. These ferocious fighters were your original tough guys. They weren't afraid of anyone —or anything! Armed with huge stone battle axes, the Vikings killed their enemies without mercy. Their combination of blood-curdling battle cries and monstrous battle axes usually meant they beat the opposition.

A more modern form of a Viking's axe was used by knights in the Middle Ages. Most knights wore a suit of metal armor to protect them in battle. It usually worked as most spears and arrows couldn't pierce it. A battle axe was the only weapon which could penetrate the armor and finish off the enemy.

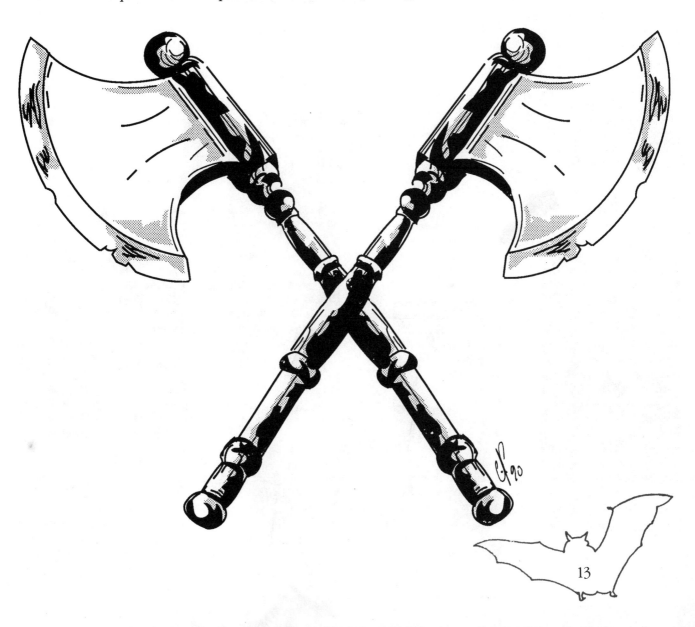

Battle Axe

Folding Instructions

1
Start with paper 2¾ × 6 inches. Fold it in half lengthwise and out again.

2
Fold the left and right sides to the middle and out again.

3
Fold both sides to the crease lines you have just made.

4
Crimp fold the top half of the model up as shown.

5
Crimp fold the top of the model down.

6
With care, cut along the dotted lines at the top. Next, fold the lower left and right sides into the middle, squash folding the tops as you go.

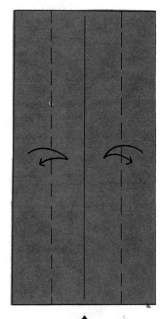

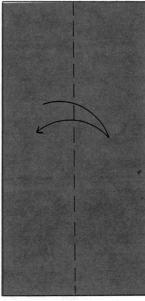

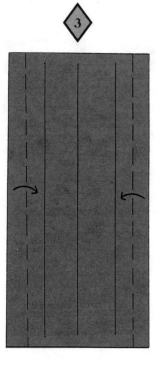

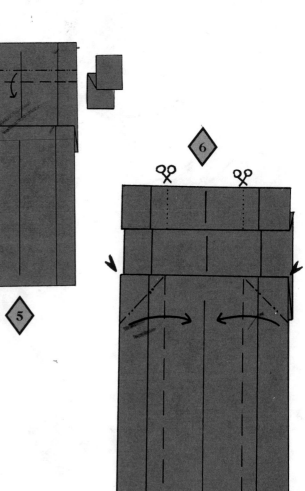

7

Fold the middle section of the top edge to a point. Fold the outer sections down. With care, cut along the dotted lines as shown.

8

Fold the two left upper corners in to meet each other. Fold the right upper corners in a little way as shown. Fold the sides of the lower section into the middle.

9

Fold the whole model in half from left to right.

10

Fold the top front flap back across to the left. Turn the model over.

11

Your battle axe is finished. Fold another axe and glue the two together to form a coat of arms.

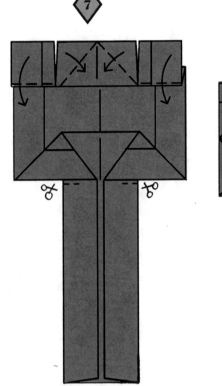

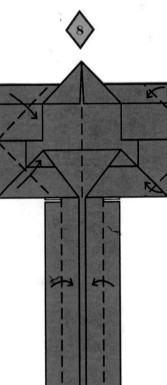

COBRA

The cobra is one of the most feared snakes in the world. It is also one of the most deadly. Cobras are found in India, some parts of Africa and the East Indies. They're famous for their "hood," which they raise just before they strike. This hood of loose skin is expanded to make the cobra look bigger and scarier. It usually works—often the sight of a cobra's hood sends predators running for cover.

Although a cobra's fangs are short, its bite is often fatal bcause it "chews" on the victim's wound. This means it can keep injecting more and more venom. Cobras feed on rats and mice, the occasional chicken or frog and sometimes other snakes. But even deadly snakes have enemies. One animal that is never fooled by the cobra's hood is a creature called the mongoose, which looks something like a weasel. It wears the snake out by "dancing" around it, never getting close enough for the cobra to strike. When the cobra starts tiring, the mongoose's sharp teeth finish it off.

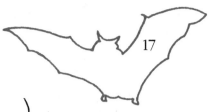
Folding Instructions

Note that the cobra diagrams are *not* to scale. The wiggly line indicates that the length has been considerably shortened.

1

Start with paper four times as long as it is wide. Fold it in half and back again.

2

Fold the four corners to the new middle crease.

3

Now fold the four new corners to the middle crease.

4

Fold the top and bottom edges to the middle.

5

Again, fold the top and bottom edges to the middle.

6

Fold the model in half, taking the top to the bottom.

7
Reverse fold the right side along the line as shown.

8
Open out the upright section by folding the inner flaps out.

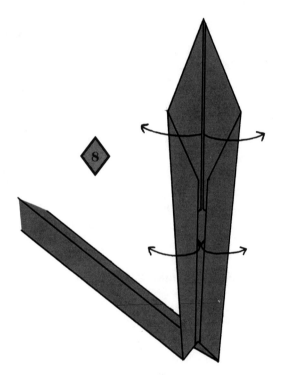

9
Bend the top point down but don't fold it flat.

10
Crimp fold the end point. Take your time with this fold.

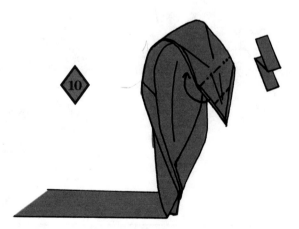

11

Press down the top of the head and fold the sides of the face under.

12

Move to the other end of the model. This will be the tail. Reverse fold the end down.

13

Reverse fold the end back up again as shown.

14

This is how the tail should look.

15

Curl the body if you will, or just leave it straight. Your cobra is finished.

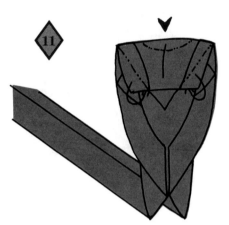

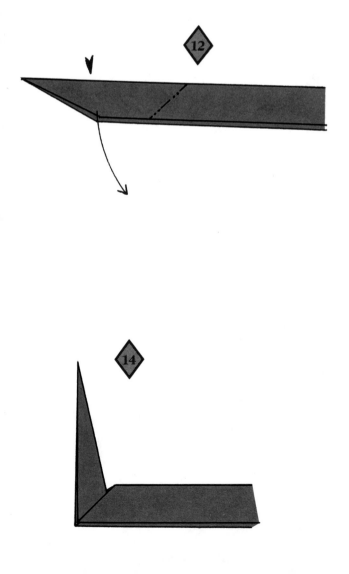

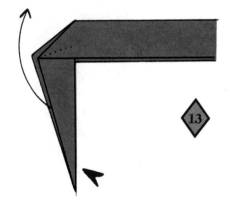

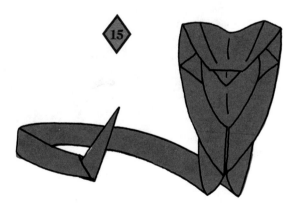

DRACULA MASK

Out of the mists of a country called Transylvania came the legend of Count Dracula – a mad nobleman who bit his victims with razor-sharp fangs and drank their blood. According to the legend, Dracula slept all day in a huge coffin. When darkness fell, he changed into a black bat and went swooping through the night in search of human blood.

Dracula's bite changed his victims. They felt weak and tired. They hated the sun. And their teeth grew longer and sharper. If the Count bit them three times, they became vampires.

Vampires were sometimes called the Undead, because although they weren't exactly alive, they could exist forever. Dracula and other vampires hated crosses, garlic and anything to do with church. The way to kill them was to drive a wooden stake through the heart before sunset.

Dracula Mask

Folding Instructions

To make this model, first fold the starter base.

1
Fold both of the front lower edges into the middle, squash folding the tops as you go.

2
Now fold the front bottom point up as shown.

3
Crimp fold the point you have just made. Take the two points at the bottom and crimp fold them up by tucking part of them under the front top section along the marked line.

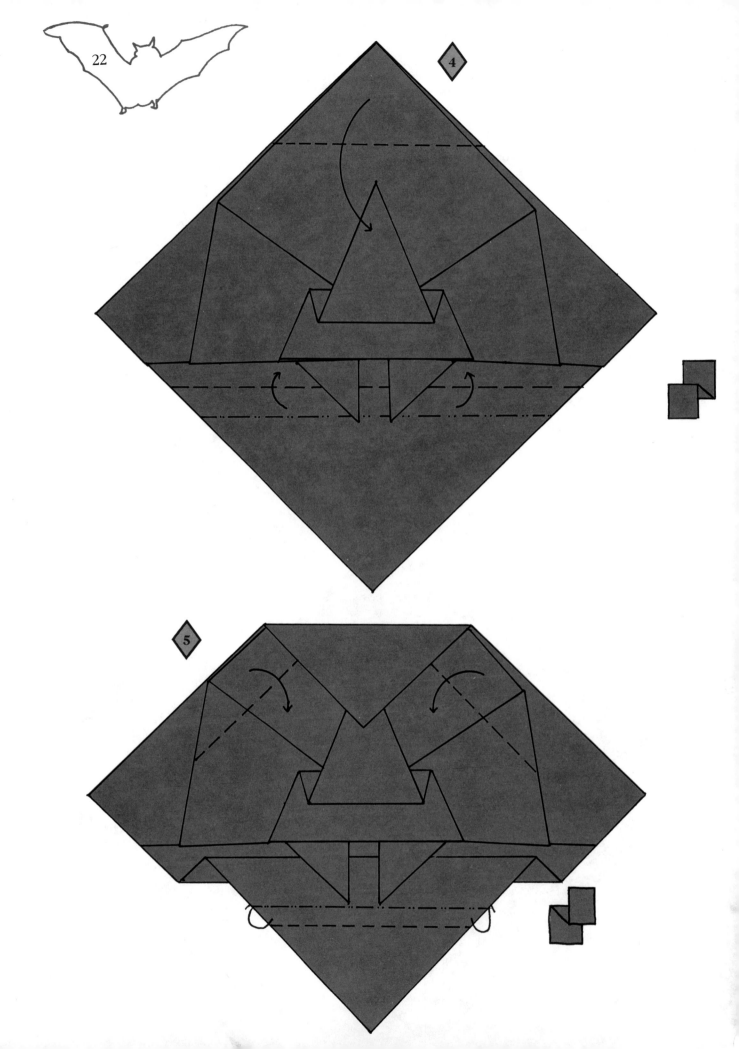

22

4

5

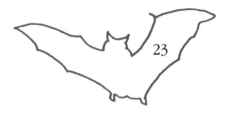

4
This is how your model should look. Fold down the very top point. Now crimp fold the lower section up under the teeth as shown.

5
With care, fold the left and right front top sections in as shown. Crimp fold the bottom section up and behind itself.

6
Fold the left and right sides behind the model along the dotted lines.

7
The finished Dracula mask. You can add to this model by coloring the areas shown.

FLYING GHOST

According to legend, ghosts are the spirits of the dead, which return to roam the earth. There are good ghosts as well as bad ones, but most ghosts are unhappy spirits trapped between this world and the next.

If someone dies before his time, or in a violent way, it is said his ghost will often be seen in the place he was killed, crying or looking lost. In England, many ghosts supposedly haunt the castles they lived in when they were alive.

Although most ghosts are just confused, some ghosts can turn violent. This sort of ghost is called a poltergeist. Poltergeists are so bitter about being ghosts that they try to destroy the living. These fearsome ghosts can throw furniture and heavy objects and make heaps of noise in order to drive away or injure humans. They also make great movie stars.

Grim Reaper

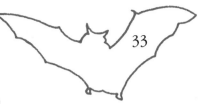

Folding Instructions

1
Start with a piece of dark paper about 8 inches square. Fold your paper in half and back again.

2
Fold down the right half along the marked line. Note the angle of the fold.

3
Now fold the point back to the right along the middle crease.

4
Fold down the left half as you did the right.

5
Now fold across the point to the left along the middle crease.

6
This is how your model should look. Turn it over.

7
Fold up the bottom left and right corners.

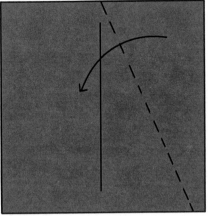

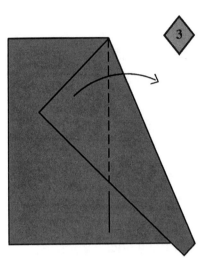

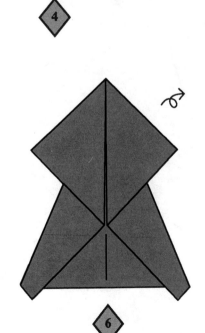

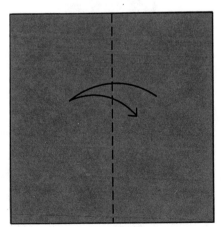

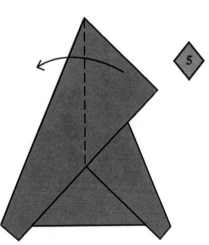

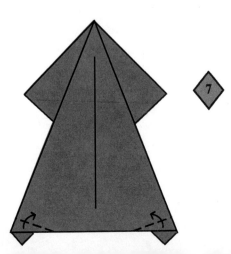

8

Fold the left and right sides into the middle crease.

9

Now fold your model in half, taking the left side behind the right.

10

Fold the front top section and the back top section down to the right on both sides of the model.

11

Now fold this same section back over itself to the right in the same way.

12

This is how your model should look. Note the folding lines. Fold in the same way as a rabbit's-ear fold to form an arm on each side of the model.

13

Push down the top section as shown to make the back of the hood. To make the hands, reverse fold up the ends of the arms and then down again. Now tuck the pointed area on the right of the model in. Repeat on the other side. Finally, fold up to the middle section on the bottom of the model.

14

Your Grim Reaper is ready.

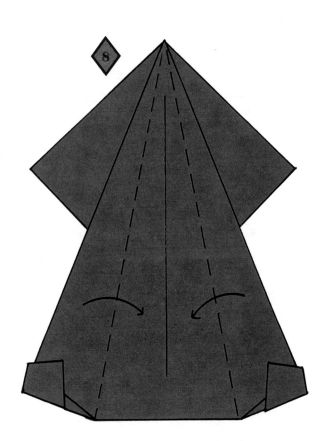

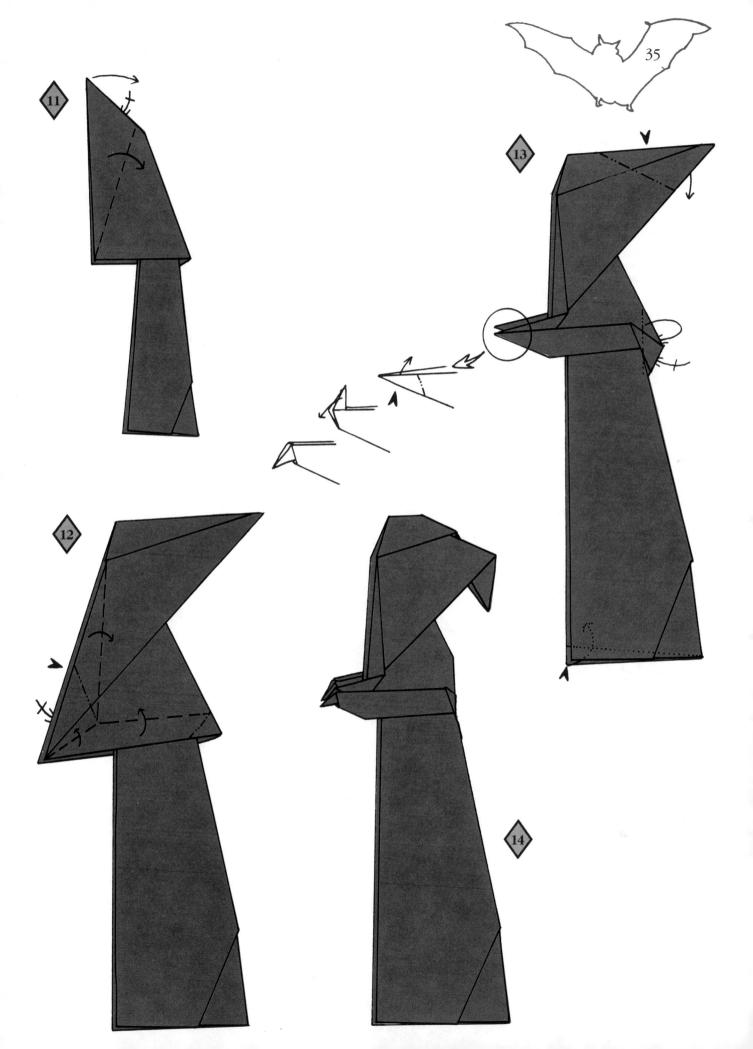

SPIDER

Huge, hairy, horrible. Is that what you think about spiders? Spiders can turn even the bravest people into cringing cowards.

But most spiders are completely harmless. They belong to a group of animals called arachnids, which means they have eight legs, two body segments and several sets of eyes. Spiders usually catch their food in sticky webs, which are strong enough to trap insects like moths, flies and small grasshoppers. Spiders are not insects.

There are only a few types of spiders whose bite is deadly. In North America we have the black widow. Hundreds of years ago, it was believed that a bite from some spiders would drive you mad. Nowadays, scientists have developed an antivenin to counteract most venomous spiders' poison.

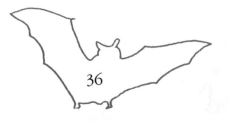

36

Spider

Folding Instructions

Spider

Start with a piece of dark colored paper 7¼ inches square. Fold this into the frog base.

1
Fold the front left flap over to the right. Repeat on the other side.

2
Fold the lower side edges into the middle. Repeat this on all three flat surfaces in the base.

3
Fold the front right flap over to the left. Repeat on the other side.

4
Reverse fold the two front bottom points up through the model.

5
This is how your model should look. Turn it over.

6
Reverse fold the two front bottom points out to the sides.

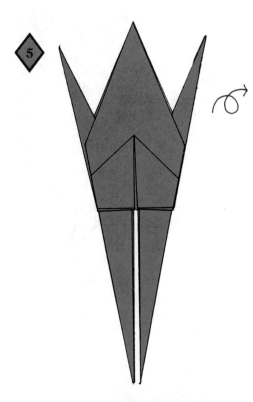

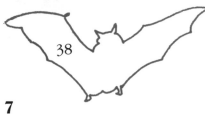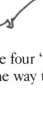

7

With care, cut the four "legs" in half along their spines all the way to the lower center of the model.

8

You should now have eight "legs." Move the four legs shown by the arrows closer to each other to make the model more symmetrical. Now fold down the top point on the body of the model.

9

Reverse fold each of the legs as shown to form joints. Fold up the point on the front of the body.

10

Now reverse fold the tips of the legs. Fold the top edges of the body under to the back as shown. Fold under the very top point. Glue the bottom section together. You may have to hold the bottom section together until it sticks.

11

Your spider is now ready.

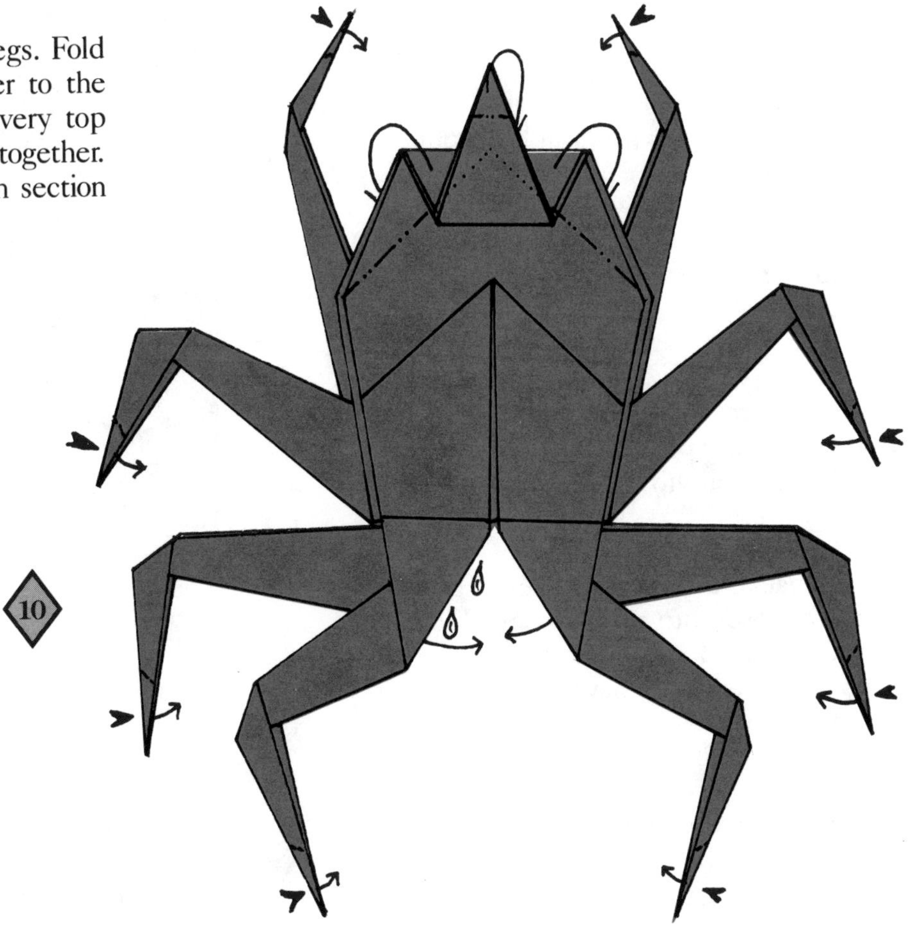

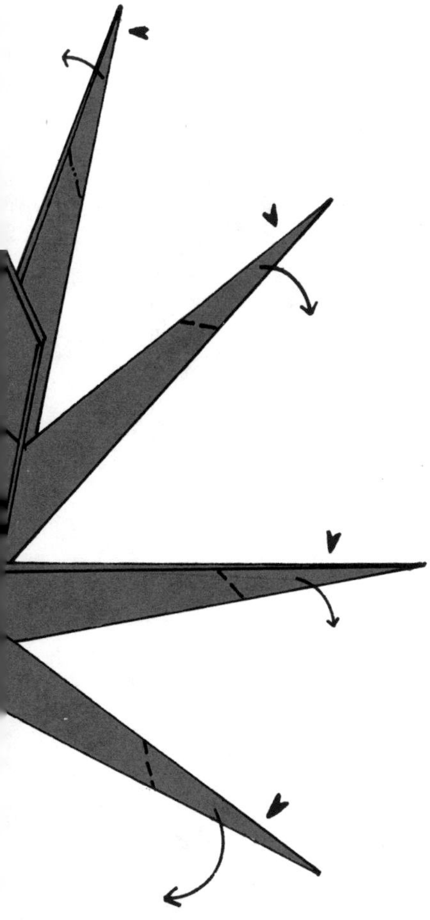

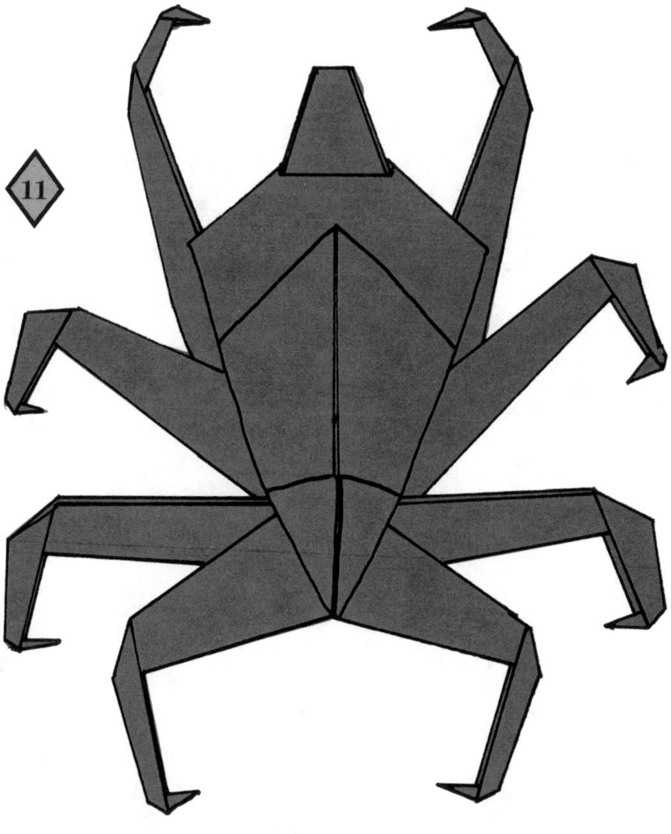

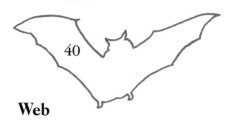

Web

1

Start with a white piece of paper 8½ inches square. Fold the paper in half from bottom to top.

2

Now fold the paper in half from left to right.

3

Fold the paper in half by taking the bottom right corner and folding it up to the top left corner and back again.

4

Note the shaded areas. With a pencil and ruler copy these onto your model. With care, take a pair of scissors and cut these areas out. When you have done this, unfold the web.

5

Place the spider you have made onto the web. You should be able to hook it onto the web without using glue.

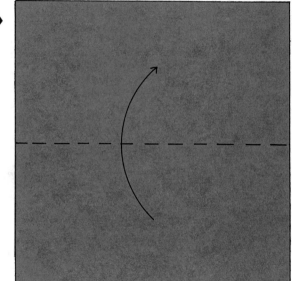

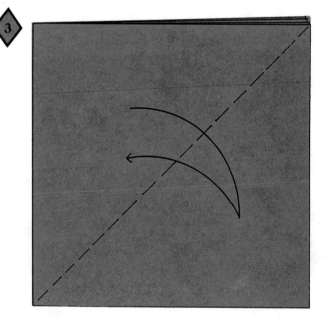

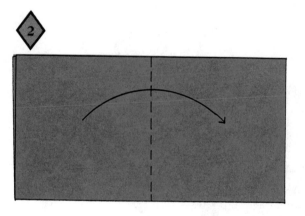

4

5

THE UNDEAD

When someone dies, they stay dead. Or do they? There are many terrifying tales of dead bodies rising – not as ghosts, but as walking, talking corpses.

Sometimes, according to the stories, a body will rise because of a promise made just before death. One such tale tells of a man who promised his wife he'd return to tell her what lay beyond the grave…and his ghastly person came shuffling to her door, the day after his death.

Others say the dead can also be made to rise. In the West Indies and parts of Africa, sorcerers practice a strange religion called voodoo. People who have recently died are made to rise as servants of the sorcerer. They walk and talk but do not feel or think. These rising corpses are known as zombies, and there are people who swear they have seen dead relatives and friends.

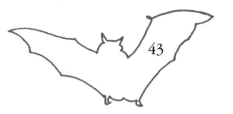

Folding Instructions

Coffin

1
These are the three sections that you will need to make up the coffin, the base and the two sides. Photocopy or trace these three sections and cut them out.

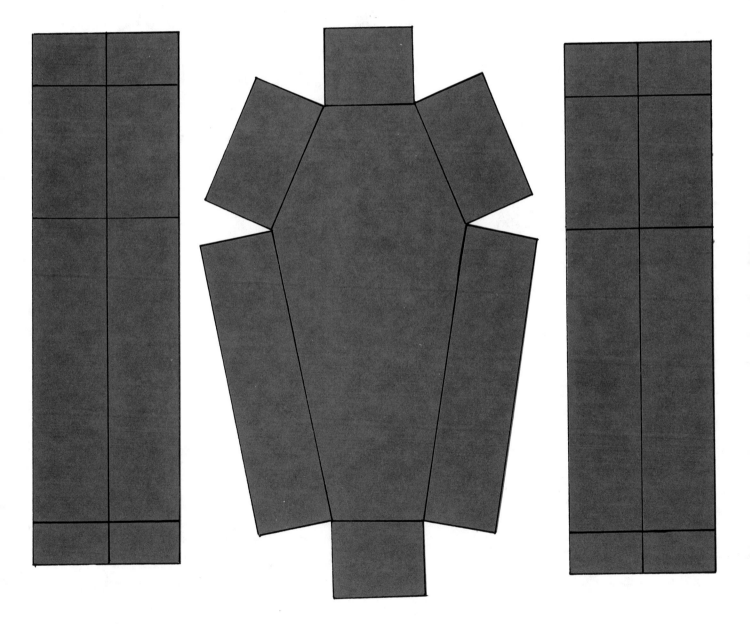

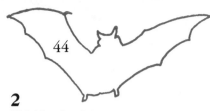

2

Fold both of the side sections in half, taking the top behind the model to the bottom, and crease them along lines shown. Fold both flaps on the coffin base up.

3

This is how your sections should look (only one side section shown). Place a drop of glue where shown and slip the side sections down over the sides of the base.

4

This is how your finished coffin should look. But where is the body?

Undead

1

Start with the bird base folded from a piece of paper 7¼ inches square. Reach in and grab the inner flaps marked.

2

Holding these flaps, pull them apart until your base is stretched out.

3

This is how your model should look. Fold the lower point up to meet the top one. You should be able to squash your model flat.

4

Rabbit's ear fold the front section down to the left. Repeat on the other side.

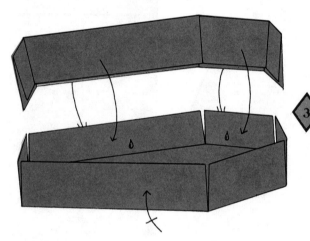

5
This is how your model should look. Take the point on the right and squash fold it down.

6
Fold this new section in half from left to right.

7
Now repeat steps 5 and 6 on the left point, but folding the new section from right to left.

8
Fold the front right flap over to the left. Repeat on the other side.

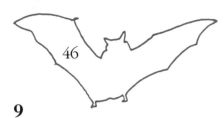

46

9

Now fold the front flap up as shown.

10

Fold the left and right edges of the top section into the middle.

11

Now fold the two lower edges into the middle as well.

12

Note the top section. This will be the head of the model. Fold it down and then each side out as shown (see the enlarged diagram). Now tuck the end point up behind the head. For the hands, crimp fold the ends of the arms in, then out, as shown in the enlarged diagrams.

13

This is how your model should look. Fold it in half from right to left.

14

Reverse fold the lower section up to the left as shown.

15

Now reverse fold the same section back up to the right as shown.

16

Open out your model.

17

Fold the arms across to the front. Now fold each side of the head back.

18

The undead is now ready to place into the coffin.

19

Just lower your undead into the coffin and . . . look out on Friday the 13th!

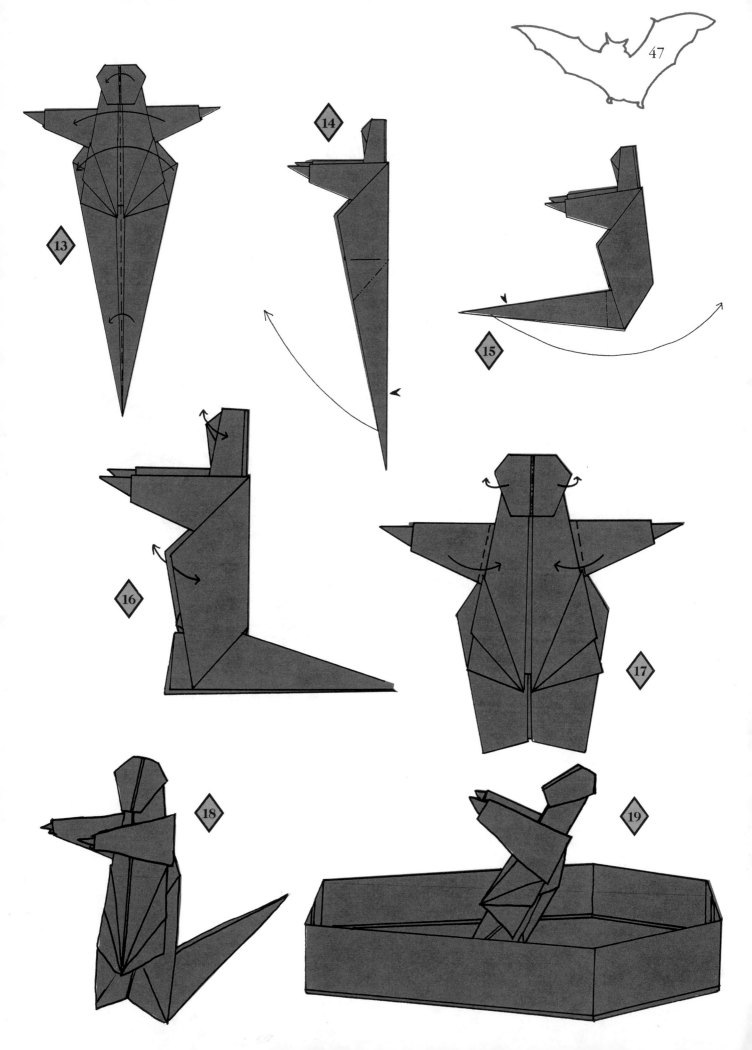

VAMPIRE BAT

The vampire bat is closely associated with the legendary blood-sucking creatures we call vampires. Many people are scared of vampire bats, but these bats usually only feed on the blood of horses and cattle. Humans are rarely bitten, and if ever, it's never on the neck. They're usually bitten on the big toe!

Vampire bats are only about 3¼ inches long. They are found in northern Mexico, Chile, Argentina and Uruguay. Like most other bats, they hang upside down in caves and trees during the daytime, only coming out at night to feed. The bats feed on their victims while they sleep, and they only bite animals in places where there are no feathers or hair.

The most dangerous thing about vampire bats isn't that they feed on blood, but that they spread diseases when they bite. Their saliva contains diseases, such as rabies, which is dangerous and can kill cattle and even humans.

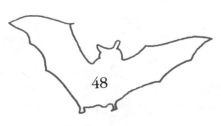

48

Vampire Bat

Folding Instructions

Start with a black square of paper.

1

Fold your paper in half diagonally. Unfold.

2

Repeat, folding on the other diagonal.

3

Fold the two top corners down to the center.

4

Note the points marked *X*. Fold these to the middle of the bottom edge at the same time squashing the topmost point to the bottom edge.

5

This is the fold halfway through.

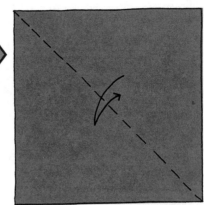

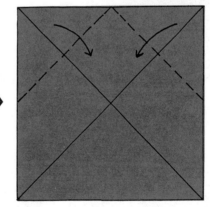

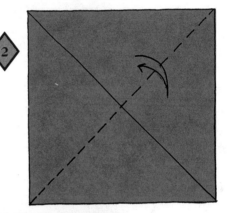

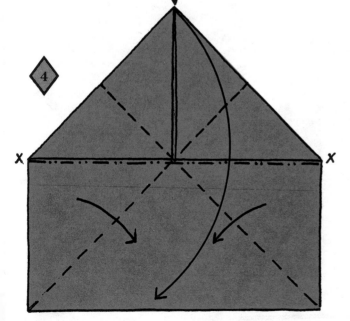

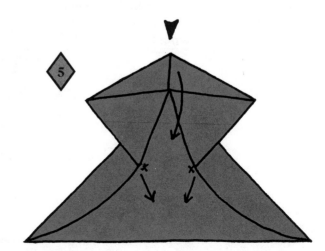

6

The finished fold. Note the area circled.

7

Squash fold the front right flap.

8

Fold up the front edge of the fold you have just made, at the same time folding the sides below it in as shown.

9

Fold down the point you have just made.

10

Now fold the front right flap across as shown.

11

Turn the model over and repeat steps 7 to 10 on the left front flap. Turn the model back over again.

12

Fold only the lower front flap up to the top.

13

Fold the top half of the model down behind the bottom half, at the same time folding the small front points up.

14

This is how your model should look. Turn it over.

15

Study the lines and arrows marked carefully. Fold the outer edges of the model down, and at the same time fold the inner edges up. You will see that the tops of the wings will squash down a little.

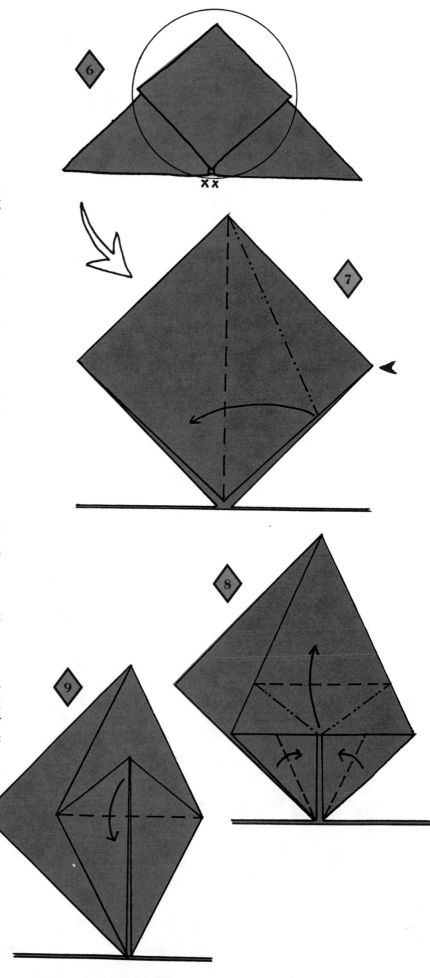

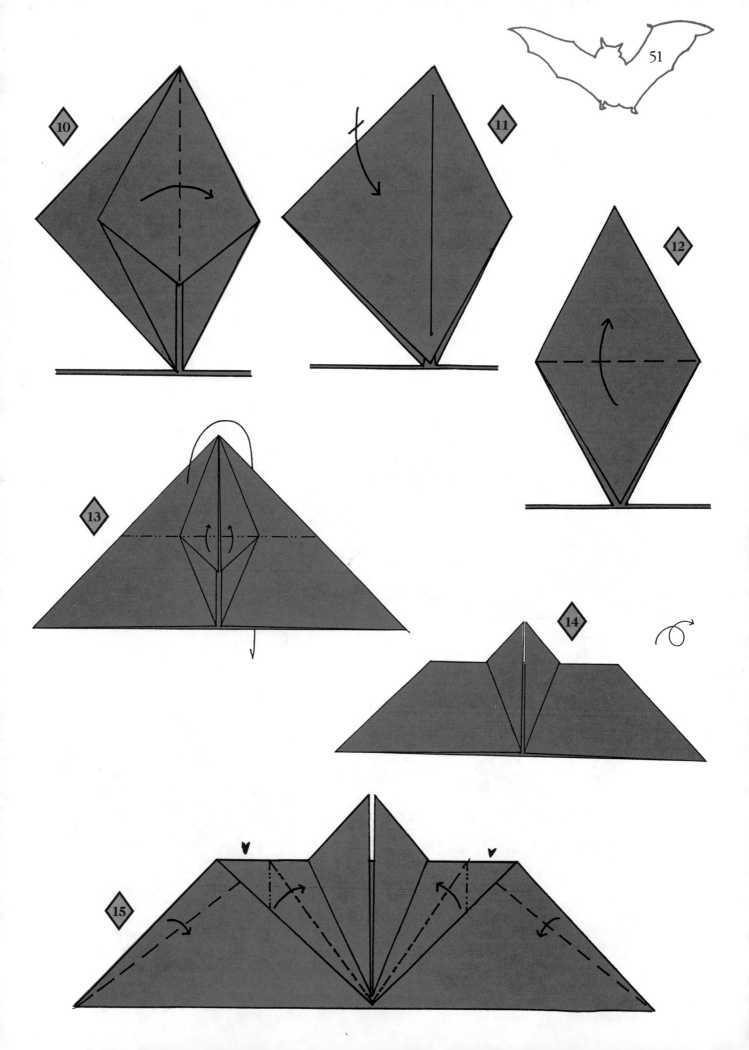

51

16

Crimp fold the ends of the wings at an angle so that the ends point down. Fold the front lower point up.

17

Now fold all the bottom edges behind the rest of the model as shown. Crimp fold the front flap in the circled area to form the nose.

18

Take the two points at the very top of the head and squash fold them down and out a little to make the ears.

19

Your vampire bat is ready to fly off and find some nice warm blood.

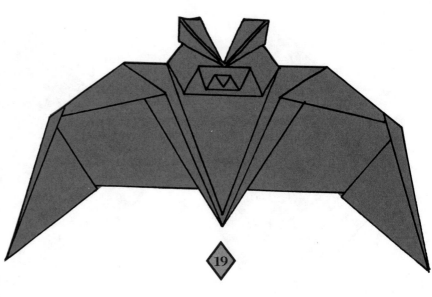

WARLOCK'S RING

The word warlock *refers to a male witch or wizard. According to the ancient meaning, a warlock was an "oath-breaker"—a man who had sold his soul to the devil in return for power over nature. The devil usually kept his promise. Warlocks often stayed young and healthy, or became rich and powerful. Many feared them, but few loved them.*

Warlocks were said to be able to make demons appear to perform certain tasks for them, or to take revenge on the warlock's enemies. Warlocks were also said to be able to look into the future and change the course of history.

But what warlocks often forgot was that they belonged to the devil. Trying to get out of the bargain was no good. A famous warlock named Faust was sorry for all the evil he had caused. He thought that this might make the devil stay away—but one night the Evil One came for him. The next morning, Faust's mangled body was found on the floor of his room.

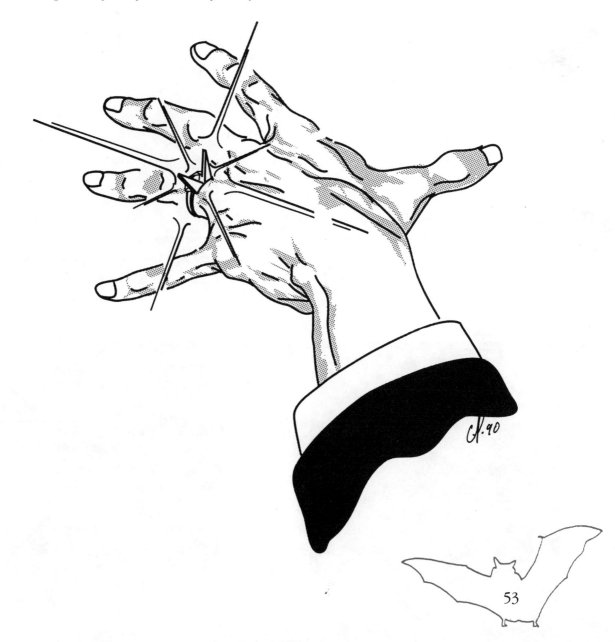

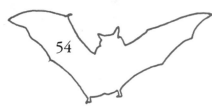

Warlock's Ring

Folding Instructions

1

Start with a 4¼-inch square of paper. Fold the paper in half from top to bottom; then unfold. Turn the paper over.

2

Now fold the paper in half, taking the top right corner to the bottom left and back again.

3

Take the top left corner and fold it to bottom right and back again.

4

Now fold the paper in half from top to bottom, bringing the points marked *X* in to meet in the center of the bottom edge.

5

This is the fold halfway through.

6

Now rabbit's ear fold the front flaps only.

7

This is how your model should look. Fold the back top point down behind the rest of the model.

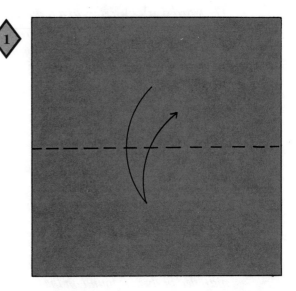

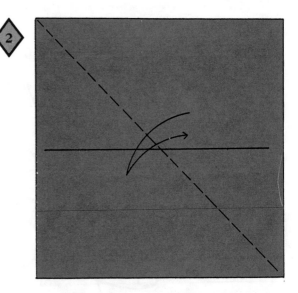

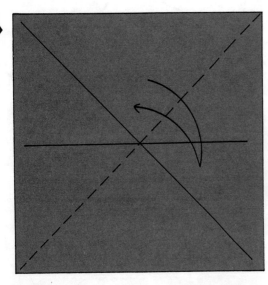

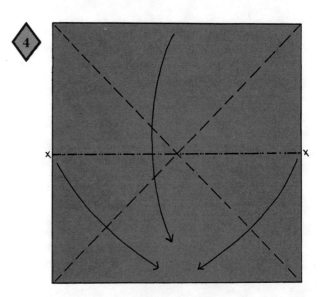

8
This is how your model should look. Turn it over.

9
Crimp fold the bottom point as shown.

10

Fold the model in half by taking the right side behind the left.

11

Fold the front top point down and up again. Repeat on the other side. Unfold the hidden right side.

12

This is how your model should look from the front. Bring the two bottom sections together.

13

Place some glue on the section shown and bring the other bottom section up, curling it around, to the glued section.

14

With the bottom sections glued, you should now be able to wear your warlock's ring.

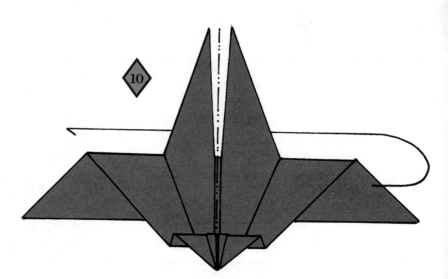

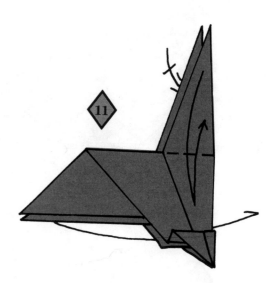

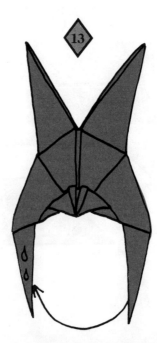

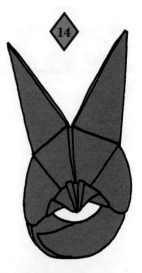

WEREWOLF

This awful beast was half-man, half-wolf and all appetite. Werewolves were ordinary people, most of the time, but when the moon was full, a horrible change came over them.

Just after sunset on a full-moon night, their hands curled into claws, their teeth lengthened into sharp fangs and fur grew over their bodies. Werewolves didn't look like wolves, or like men. They were a hideous combination of both, with a wolf's killer instinct and a man's intelligence.

On full-moon nights, so legend has it, many animals and people were killed by the strange hairy beast. Most folk would lock their doors at this time. The only way to kill a werewolf was to track it back to its house, wait until night and shoot it with a silver bullet. Anyone unlucky enough to be bitten by a werewolf would become one.

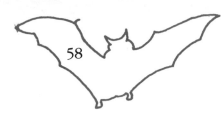

Werewolf

Folding Instructions

To make the werewolf you will need two pieces of paper the same color.

Head

1
Start with a 3¼-inch square of paper. Fold it in half diagonally, then unfold.

2
Now fold your paper along the other diagonal, then unfold.

3
Take the left and right corners and fold them into the center.

4
Fold these same corners out again along the marked lines.

5
This is how your model should look. Turn it over.

6
Fold each of the four corners in along the lines shown.

7
Fold the model in half from top to bottom.

8
Now fold the model in half from left to right.

9
Take the front lower flap and fold it up along the marked line. Repeat on the other side. These will be the ears. Pull the upper and lower jaws apart a little.

10
This is how the head should be looking. Note the area circled.

11
Reverse fold the point of the upper jaw back over the jaw and fold the point of the lower jaw under and inside it.

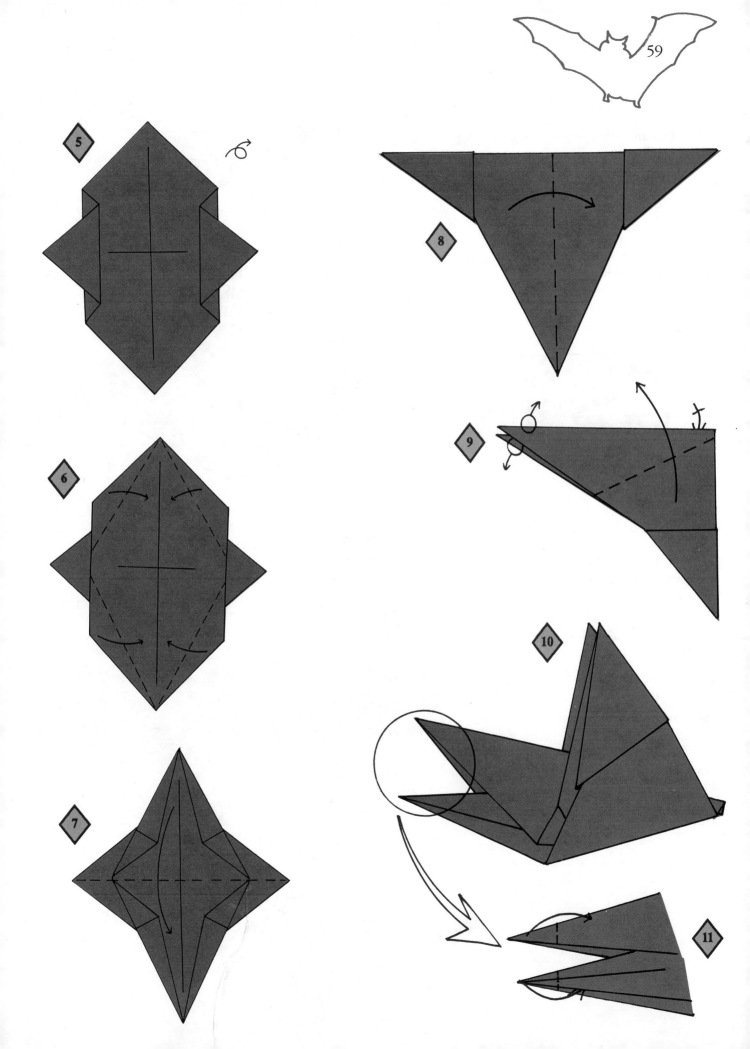

12

To form the nose, reverse fold the top point to the left as shown.

13

Tuck the tip under and into the top jaw.

14

This is how your finished head should look. Now to make the body.

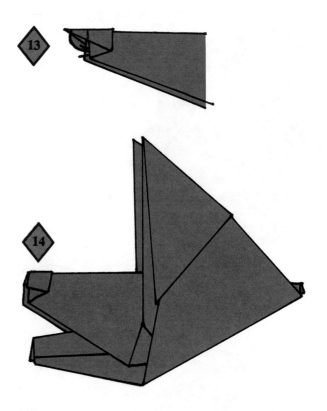

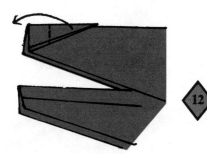

Body

Start with a bird base folded from an 8½-inch square of paper.

1

Reach in and grab the two inner flaps marked.

2

Holding these flaps, pull them apart until your base is stretched out.

3

This is how your model should look. Fold the lower point up to meet the top one. You should be able to squash your model flat.

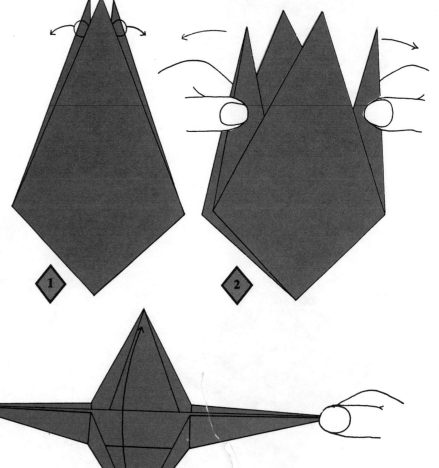

4
Rabbit's ear fold the front section down to the left. Turn your model over, repeat on the other side and turn your model back again.

5
This is how your model should look. Squash fold the right point down.

6
Fold this new section in half, from left to right.

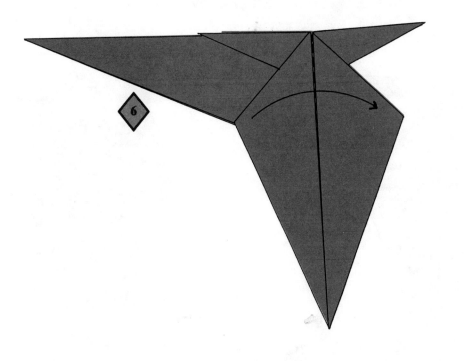

62

7

Now repeat steps 5 and 6 on the left point.

8

Fold the front right over to the left. Repeat on the other side (remember to turn your model over and then back again).

9

Now fold the front flap up as shown.

10

Cut along the dotted line on the lower section. Turn the model over.

11

Fold the sides of the lower section in as shown.

12

Fold the model in half from right to left.

13

Reverse fold the two lower sections up to the right.

14

Now reverse fold these same sections down to the left.

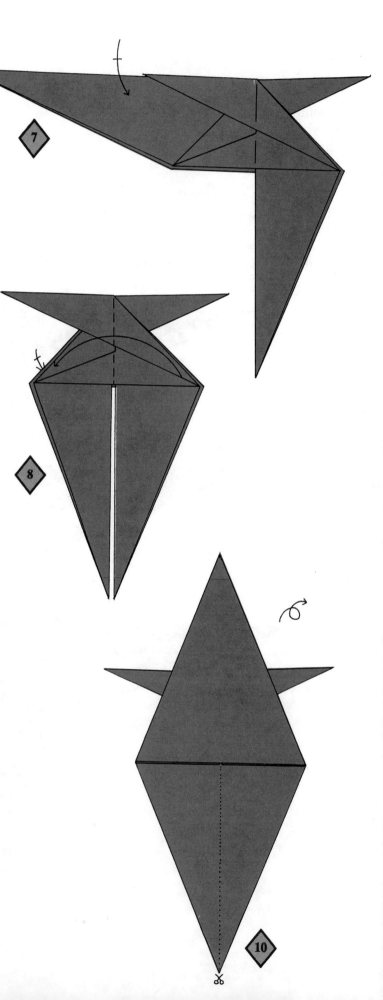

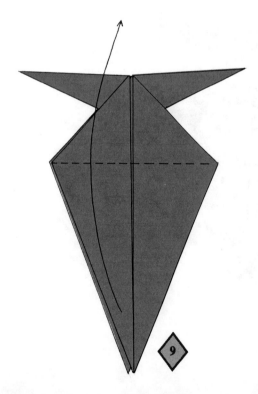

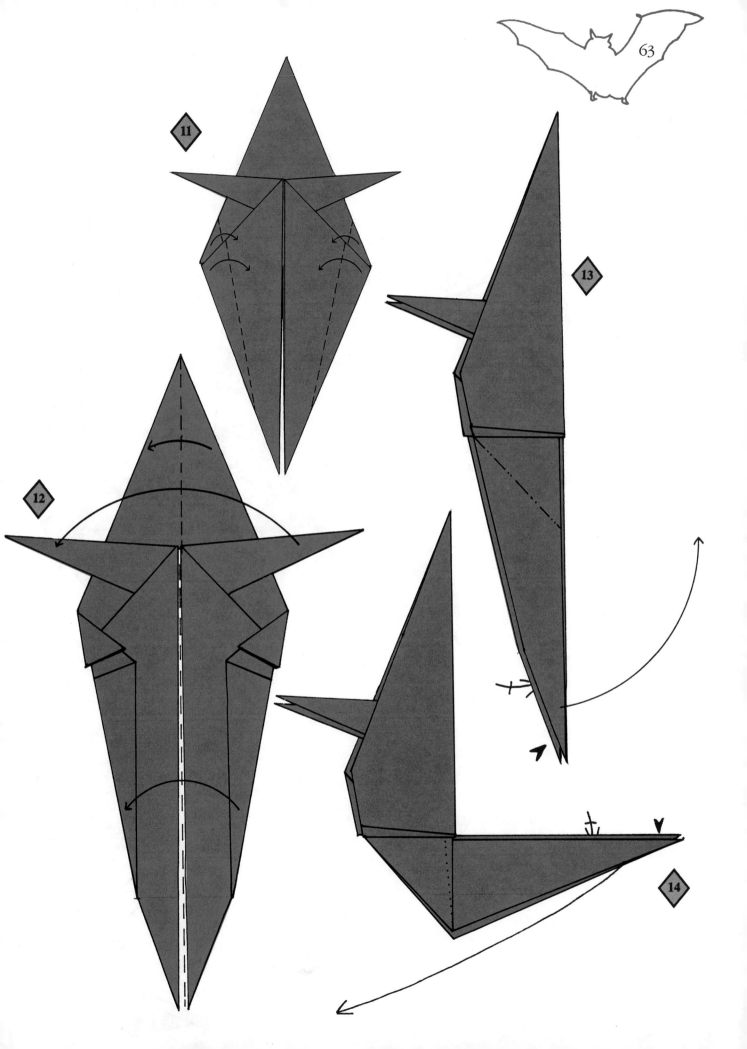

15
To make the neck, reverse fold the top point down into itself. Now fold the front left point into the neck. Repeat on the other side. To make the hands, reverse fold the ends of the legs to the right and then back again to the left. Tuck in the four points on the back of the legs.

16
Now your body is finished. Place some glue on the top of the neck and glue on the head.

17
The finished werewolf. Watch out for the next full moon and keep your silver bullets handy!

INDEX